This edition copyright
© 1999 Lion Publishing
Illustrations copyright
© 1999 Pip Adams

Published by
Lion Publishing plc
Sandy Lane West, Oxford,
England
www.lion-publishing.co.uk
ISBN 0 7459 4171 0

First edition 1999
10 9 8 7 6 5 4 3 2 1 0

Acknowledgments

p. 16: reprinted with
permission from Everyman's
Library, David Campbell
Publishers.

p. 22: from The Authorized
Version of the Bible (The
King James Bible), the rights
in which are vested in the
Crown, reproduced by
permission of the Crown's
Patentee, Cambridge
University Press.

Every effort has been made
to trace and acknowledge
copyright holders of all the
quotations in this book. We
apologize for any errors or
omissions that may remain,
and would ask those
concerned to contact the
publishers, who will ensure
that full acknowledgment
is made in the future.

A catalogue record for this
book is available from the
British Library

Typeset in 16/20 Kidprint
Printed and bound in
Singapore

Now you're a Dad!

Compiled by Emma Fox

LION
Hudson

Now you're a Dad!

So now you're a dad.

If you're anything like the dads in this book, you'll probably be feeling a strange combination of joy, shock and blind terror. You'll also – and this is a feeling which will grow and grow – feel love. A bit of a miracle, perhaps, amidst the sleepless nights, interesting smells and indescribable nappies.

(And this is only
the beginning...)
Now you're a dad,
you'll give more than you have
ever given before. But you'll
also have the sheer delight of
receiving it all back, and more.
And now you're a dad,
you can just begin to imagine
something of the love that
God, the ultimate 'dad', feels
for you.

The very words
'my father'
make me smile.

Angela Carter

Safety; nothing could get at me if I curled up on my father's lap, holding onto his ear, with one thumb tucked into it... All about him was safe.

Naomi Mitchison

Before I got married I had six theories about bringing up children; now I have six children and no theories.

Lord Rochester

He threw his jelly
and cream all over Dad,
then laughed and clapped.

Adrian Plass

Parents learn a lot
from children about
coping with life.

Muriel Spark

I sang my child to sleep
And her sweet sleep
Breathed like a flower on m
A peace so deep
That I did share her balm
And know her rest.
Sweet, in thy blessing sleep
I too am blessed.

Margaret Ruddock

You should have seen Dad when I came down the next morning. He looked like a dead walrus. The triplets were cackling and chattering and crawling and dribbling all over him.

'Good night, Dad?' I said.

Poor old Dad was just a grey lump with a grey voice.

'No, Gerald,' he said faintly, 'I did not have a good night.'

Adrian Plass

We can't form our children
on our own concepts;
we must take them
and love them as
God gives them to us.

Johann Wolfgang von Goethe

Allow children to be happy
in their own way, for what
better way will they find?

Samuel Johnson

Fathers, provoke not
your children to anger,
lest they be discouraged.

**From the New Testament
letter to the Colossians**

If the new father feels bewildered and even defeated, let him take comfort from the fact that whatever he does in any fathering situation has a fifty per cent chance of being right.

Bill Cosby

We never know the love
of our parents until we
become parents ourselves.

Henry Ward Beecher

Every time you pick your baby up, even if you do it a little awkwardly at first, every time you change her, bathe her, feed her, smile at her, she's getting a feeling that she belongs to you and that you belong to her. Nobody else in the world... can give that to her.

Benjamin Spock

The son has absolutely no idea of what the father is going through until he becomes a father himself.

Tony Parsons

You are going to know this person better than you will ever know anybody else.

Penelope Leach

He that will have his son
have a respect for him...
must himself have a great
reverence for his son.

John Locke

We know for a fact that the natural loving care that kindly parents give their children is a hundred times more valuable than their knowing how to pin a diaper on just right.

Benjamin Spock

Feel the dignity of
a child. Do not feel
superior to him,
for you are not.

Robert Harris

Your children are
not your children.
They come through you
but not from you.

Kahlil Gibran

You have kids, you put 'em
on their feet and they go.
Your job is to help them
become independent.
You don't have them
to hold onto them.

Parent of five

I was never very good with children... How were you supposed to talk to them? What did you **do** with them...? Now I had my own child. How would I behave?

Peter Howarth

It is a wise father
that knows his own child.

William Shakespeare

If you're a parent, you turn yourself over to thoughts of someone else for ever.

Parent of four

He makes me laugh
and I feel through him
that the world can *be*
a wonderful place.

Peter Howarth

[Getting home after the birth]

The previous day I'd been overwhelmed by a sense of relief that it was all over. Now I realized that it was just about to begin.

Peter Howarth

Most of us become parents
long before we have
stopped being children.

Mignon McLaughlin

The only thing that prevented a father's love from faltering was the fact that there was in his possession a photograph

f himself at the same early

ige, in which he, too, looked

like a homicidal fried egg.

P.G. Wodehouse

Parenting will
eventually produce
bizarre behaviour,
and I'm not talking
about the kids.

Bill Cosby

Playing with children is a glorious thing, but I have never understood why it is considered a soothing or idyllic one. It reminds me not of watering little budding flowers, but of wrestling for hours with gigantic angels and devils.

G.K. Chesterton

What a father says to
his children is not heard
by the world, but it will
be heard by posterity.

Jean Paul Richter

If men do not keep
on speaking terms with
children, they cease to be
men, and become merely
machines for eating and
for earning money.

John Updike

Sometimes a father is so eager to have his son turn out perfect that it gets in the way of their having a good time together.

Benjamin Spock

The love I feel for him
is like a physical ache.

Peter Howarth

Changing nappies is fine
for now, I thought, but
eventually he'll need the kind
of guidance and leadership
that can only really come

from a grown-up. Will I
have to hire someone?
I'm willing to learn, but
there may not be time.

Tim Dowling

What kids want is a dad.
And dads, by definition,
are not cool.

Neil Spencer

Tenderness, gentleness and kindness are the building blocks in a child's soul. They equip the child to hear the whisper of God when he says, 'I love you.'

Mike Yaconelli